The Chicken Master

Chicken Akademy

Table of Contents

Recipes

CHICKEN FRIED STEAK

ingredients

- 2 lb. beef round steak
- 1 egg, beaten
- 1 tbsp. milk
- 1 c. crushed saltine crackers

Salt & pepper to taste Cooking oil for frying

directions

1. Punch steak with knife, cut into chunks for serv-ing.
2. Blend the egg and milk. Mix the cookie crumbs, salt and pepper on a separate plate.
3. Dip the meat in the egg mixture and then in the cookies.
4. Brown the meat on both sides in hot oil, then lower the heat to a simmer, cover the pan and cook until tender for 40-45 minutes. Meat sauce: Remove meat when done from skillet, add a little water / flour mixture to fat.
5. Bring to a boil. Then simmer until you get the desired consistency.

ITALIAN CHICKEN

ingredients

- 1 frying chicken, cut up
- 2 tbsp.
- Melted butter Salt & pepper
- 2 tbsp. dry Italian salad dressing mix
- 1 can condensed mushroom soup
- 2 (3 oz.) pkg. cream cheese (cut into cubes)

directions

1. Wash the chicken and pat dry. Brush with butter.
2. Sprinkle with salt and pepper.
3. Place in a slow cooker.
4. Sprinkle with dry salad mix.
5. Cover and simmer for 5-6 hours. About 3/4 hours before serving, mix the soup and cream cheese.

SO EASY OVEN - FRIED CHICKEN

ingredients

- 1 frying chicken, cut into
- 8 pieces
- 1/4 lb.
- Melted butter
- 1/8 tsp. garlic powder
- 1/8 tsp. paprika
- 1/8 tsp. thyme
- 1 tsp. salt
- 1 1/2 c. dry bread crumbs, finely crushed cornflakes or flour

directions

1. Dip the chicken pieces in butter, then toss in a paper bag containing the remaining dry ingredients.
2. Place skin side up in lightly greased 9 x 13-inch baking dish and bake for 50 minutes at 350 degrees or until done. Serves 6-8.

MEXICAN CHICKEN CASSEROLE

ingredients

- 6 chicken breast or 1 whole chicken
- 1 can cream of mushroom soup
- 10 oz. Velveeta cheese
- 1 can Rotel tomatoes
- 1 c. milk
- 1 bag Doritos

directions

1. Boil the chicken. Bone and chop the chicken.
2. Combine milk, Velveeta, soup, and tomatoes; bring to a boil.
3. Add the meat and simmer for 5 to 10 minutes, stirring frequently.
4. Place a layer of Doritos in a long saucepan, then layer with the meat mixture.

SOUR CREAM AND CHICKEN ENCHILADAS

ingredients

- 6 boneless chicken breast
- 8 flour tortillas
- 8 oz. sour cream
- 1 jar picante sauce
- 2 c. Monterey Jack cheese

directions

1. Boil the chicken breast.
2. Cut in slices. Simmer chicken in hot sauce. Lightly butter the flour tortillas.
3. Fill the tortillas with the chicken mixture. Place the open side upside down in a saucepan.
4. Cut slices on top of the tortillas.
5. Spread sour cream and then cheese on top of tortillas.
6. Bake at 350 degrees for about 30 minutes until cheese is melted.

CHICKEN CASSEROLE

ingredients

- 1 can Rotel tomatoes with chilies
- 1 can cream of mushroom soup
- 1 sm. Velveeta cheese, diced
- 1 sm. onion, sauteed
- 1 stick margarine
- 1 whole chicken
- 1 c. Cheddar cheese
- 1 pack spaghetti

directions

1. Boil the chicken and remove the bone. In the same water, boil the spaghetti and drain, but do not rinse.
2. Mix all ingredients except Cheddar cheese.
3. Bake at 350 degrees until Velveeta cheese is melted and hot. Garnish with cheddar cheese and serve.

CHICKEN SPAGHETTI

ingredients

- 5 chicken breasts
- 1 can cream of chicken soup
- 1 (8 oz.) pkg. Velveeta, grated
- 1 (8 oz.) pkg. spaghetti noodles

directions

1. Boil the chicken with the skin intact, approximately 25 minutes, with salt and pepper.
2. Remove the boiled chicken, remove the skin and bone. Boil the spaghetti in the broth. Spray a 9 x 13-inch pan with Pam.
3. Place chicken pieces, soup, cheese, 1 1/2 cups chicken broth, and cooked spaghetti in a skillet and bake at 350 degrees for 35 minutes.

THYME CHICKEN

ingredients

- 4 boneless chicken breasts
- 1/2 pt. whipping cream
- 1 stick butter Thyme
- Salt & pepper to taste Sliced fresh mushrooms

directions

1. Melt the stick of butter in a skillet. Wash and dry the chicken. Fry the chicken in butter until golden. Take out the chicken and sprinkle with thyme.
2. Sauté the mushrooms in butter. Return the chicken to the pan with the mushrooms and pour the cream over them.
3. Cook until cream thickens and browns. This is delicious served with a rice casserole and a green bean casserole.

CHICKEN POT PIE

ingredients

- 2 pie shells
- 2 cans mixed vegetables

Whole chicken

- 1 stick butter

directions

1. Take the chicken and boil it until done.
2. Put 1 cake in the bottom of a deep bowl. Remove the chicken from the bones. Then mix the chicken, chicken broth with mixed greens and butter. Then pour over the cake base. Then place the other pie crust on top.
3. Bake for 45 minutes at 325 degrees.

MOZZARELLA CHICKEN AND SAUCE

ingredients

- 4 chicken breast with or without bones
- 1 jar Ragu spaghetti sauce (tomatoes and herbs)
- 1/2 green bell pepper, chopped
- 1 sm. onion, chopped
- 1/4 c. sliced ham, chopped
- 1 c. mozzarella cheese Dales steak sauce
- Salt, pepper & garlic powder to taste

directions

1. Cover bottom of Pyrex (Bakeware) Dish with Dales Steak Sauce. Cover the bottom of the plate with the chicken (brown it optional).
2. Sprinkle the chicken with onion, green bell pepper, salt, pepper, garlic powder, and ham.
3. Cover with Ragu sauce.
4. Cover and cook for 50 minutes in a preheated oven, baking temperature of 350 degrees.
5. Remove the lid and top with cheese. Continue cooking until the cheese is melted, about 5 minutes. Serve over spaghetti and with French bread. Makes 4 servings as a full meal.

CHICKEN WITH MOZZARELLA CHEESE

ingredients

- 6 chicken breasts
- 3 eggs, beaten & salted Progresso bread crumbs
- 2 tbsp.
- Melted butter
- 4 tbsp.
- Cooking oil
- 1 (10 1/2 oz.) can cream of chicken soup
- 1 c. chicken broth
- 8 oz. mozzarella cheese slices

directions

1. Dip the chicken pieces in beaten eggs, roll in the breadcrumbs and brown in oil and butter.
2. Place in a saucepan.
3. Combine the soup and broth.
4. Pour over chicken and bake covered at 350 degrees for 30 minutes.
5. Place the cheese slices on the chicken and bake 10 more minutes uncovered. Serve with rice.

SWISS CHEESE CHICKEN CASSEROLE

ingredients

- 4-6 chicken breasts
- 6 slices Swiss cheese
- 1 can cream of mushroom soup
- 1/4 c. milk
- 2 c. Pepperidge Farm herb seasoning stuffing mix
- 1/4 c. margarine

directions

1. Place the chicken in a lightly greased casserole.
2. Place the cheese on top of the chicken.
3. Mix soup and milk; pour over chicken.
4. Cover the mixture with the filling mixture. Drizzle butter over the crumbs.
5. Cover and bake at 350 degrees for 50 minutes.

CHICKEN DIVAN

ingredients

- 1 can cream of chicken soup
- 1 (8 oz.) pkg. sour cream
- 8 oz. shredded Cheddar cheese
- 4-6 chicken breasts
- 3/4 c. chicken broth Bread crumbs Butter or margarine
- 1 bunch fresh broccoli or lg. pkg. frozen

directions

1. Preheat the oven to 375 degrees. Boil and bone the chicken. Reserve 3/4 cup of the broth.
2. Place raw broccoli in bottom of 8 1/2 x 11-inch saucepan.
3. Top with chicken pieces. In a small bowl, combine the soup, sour cream, and chicken broth.
4. Pour over the chicken.
5. Top with cheese.
6. Sprinkle with breadcrumbs and sprinkle with butter. Bake about 1 minute until cheese is golden.

CHEESE N CHICKEN ENCHILADAS

ingredients

- 1 med. onion, chopped
- 2 tbsp. margarine
- 1 1/2 c. shredded cooked chicken
- 1 jar picante sauce
- 8 flour tortillas (6)
- 1 pkg. (3 oz.) cream cheese

directions

1. cubed
2. 1 tsp. ground cumin
3. 2 c. shredded extra sharp Cheddar cheese”

CHICKEN AND BROCCOLI CASSEROLE

ingredients

- 4 chicken breast fillets
- 1 lb. broccoli, frozen
- 1 can cream of mushroom soup
- 1 can cream of chicken soup
- 1 (8 oz.) Velveeta cheese
- 1/2 box Ritz crackers

directions

1. Cut the chicken fillets into small pieces.
2. Sauté in butter until it turns white.
3. Cook the broccoli according to the directions on the package.
4. Mix in the chicken and broccoli.
5. Place in 8 x 8 inch saucepan.
6. Melt the Velveeta cheese in the microwave.
7. Add both cans of soup to the cheese.
8. Pour over the chicken and broccoli.
9. Stir until well mixed.
10. Top with crushed Ritz crackers.
11. Bake at 350 degrees for about 30 minutes until golden brown.

CHICKEN LALA PIE

ingredients

- 1 pkg. family size chicken
- 1 (8 oz.) sour cream
- 1 pkg. Stove Top stuffing
- 1/2 stick butter
- 1 (8 oz.) can cream of mushroom soup

directions

1. Preparation time: 400 degrees.
2. Cooking time: 45 minutes. Boil the chicken, let it cool and bone. Chop the chicken into small pieces. Place in the bottom of a saucepan.
3. Mix sour cream and cream of mushroom cream and spread over chicken.
4. Use 3 cups of broth (leftover from boiling chicken), 1/2 stick of butter, let butter melt.
5. Mix the seasonal mix from the stuffing box into the broth. Then blend the filling.
6. Spread over the top of the casserole.
7. Bake at 400 degrees for 45 minutes.

CHICKEN TETRAZZINI

ingredients

- 1 chicken
- 8 oz. vermicelli
- 1/2 c. chopped bell pepper
- 1 lg. chopped onion
- 2 cans mushroom soup
- 1/4 tsp. celery salt
- 1/2 tsp. black pepper
- 1 tbsp. Worcestershire sauce
- 3/4 lb. Cheddar cheese, grated

directions

1. Remove the chicken from the bone and cut it into small pieces.
2. Cook the bell pepper and onion in 1 cup of chicken broth.
3. Cook the noodles in the rest of the broth very slowly.
4. Mix all ingredients.
5. Heat 25 minutes at 350 degrees.

CHICKEN AND BISCUITS

ingredients

- 3 tbsp. margarine
- 3 chicken breasts, cooked & boned
- 3 tbsp. chopped onion
- 3 tbsp. chopped celery
- 2 tbsp. Worcestershire sauce
- 2/3 drops Tabasco
- Salt & pepper to taste
- 1 can (10 count) Hungry Jack buttermilk biscuits
- 1 sm. can 1 can cream of mushroom or chicken soup
- 1/2 c. sour cream
- 1/2 c. milk
- 2 c. grated Cheddar cheese

directions

1. Cut the chicken into very small pieces. In a skillet, melt the margarine and sauté the onion and celery.
2. Add Worcestershire sauce, Tabasco, salt and pepper.
3. Add cut chicken to this mixture. In a bowl, combine the soup, sour cream, and milk; set aside. Using a rolling pin, roll out each cookie until it is flat.
4. Put a tablespoon of chicken mixture on each cookie, fold the cookie and bring all the edges together.
5. Place cookies in a lightly greased baking dish and bake for 10-15 minutes at 400 degrees or until light golden brown.
6. Remove from the oven and top with the soup mixture and shredded cheese and return to the oven for 10-15 minutes until the cheese and soup are bubbly.

Breast CHICKEN POT PIE

ingredients

- 4 chicken breasts
- 1 can cream of chicken soup
- 1 c. chicken broth
- 1 c. milk
- 1 bag frozen peas & carrots
- 5-6 boiled eggs
- Salt & pepper to taste
- 1 stick of butter
- 1 can flaky biscuits (10 ct.)

directions

1. Boil the chicken until done.
2. Cook the peas and carrots.
3. Mix 1 can of cream of chicken, broth, milk, melted butter, salt and pepper. Cook over low heat until the sauce thickens. Then layer chicken, gravy, veggies, hard-boiled eggs, gravy, and crackers. Separate cookies and cover completely.
4. Bake according to directions or cookies until golden brown.

SWEET & SOUR CHICKEN

ingredients

- 2 pkg. boneless chicken
- 2 bell peppers
- 1 lg. onion
- 1 tbsp. flour
- 2 jars Sweet & Sour Sauce
- 1 c. flour
- 1 c. oil
- Salt & pepper as desired

directions

1. Heat 1 cup of oil. Wash the chicken pieces and pat dry, salt and pepper to taste.
2. Roll the chicken in a cup of flour and fry until crisp.
3. Remove and drain. Drain all but a small amount of oil from the pan and sauté the onion and bell pepper for 5 minutes.

CHICKEN BREAST CASSEROLE

ingredients

- 8 chicken breast
- 1 can cream of chicken soup
- 1 tbsp. grated onion
- 1 tbsp. lemon juice
- 3 tbsp. mayonnaise
- 1/2 c. slivered almonds (optional)

directions

1. Cook chicken breast until tender.
2. Remove the skin and bones and cut the chicken breast in half.
3. Mix the sauce and place the breast in a Pyrex dish. Leave space between the breasts.
4. Put sauce on each breast separately. Just before baking, top with crushed potato chips or Ritz crackers or cornflakes.
5. Bake at 400 degrees for 20 minutes.

CHICKEN AND BROCCOLI CASSEROLE

ingredients

- 2 c.
- Cooked, chopped chicken
- 2 (10 oz.) pkgs. frozen broccoli
- 2 cans cream of chicken soup
- 3/4 c. mayonnaise
- 1/2 tsp. lemon juice
- 1/2 tsp. curry powder
- 1/2 c. grated cheese or more
- 1/2 c. Pepperidge Farm stuffing mix or more

directions

1. Cook the broccoli until tender in salted water.
2. Put in a large baking dish.
3. Place the cooked and chopped chicken on top of the broccoli.
4. Combine soup, lemon juice, curry, and mayonnaise.
5. Mix well. Spread over chicken.
6. Top with cheese.
7. Sprinkle with filling mixture.
8. Bake at 350 degrees for 25 to 30 minutes.

BUSY DAY CHICKEN & RICE

ingredients

- 1 c. uncooked rice
- 1 chicken, cut up
- 1 stick oleo
- 1 pkg. dry onion soup mix
- 4 c. boiling water
- Salt & pepper to taste

directions

1. Preheat the oven to 350 degrees. Grease the bottom of a 13x9 ”x2” pan.
2. Cover the bottom evenly with rice. Place the chicken pieces on the rice. Drizzle with oil or margarine.
3. Sprinkle dried onion soup on top. Salt and pepper to taste.
4. Pour boiling water over everything.
5. Bake 1 hour. If you want a more browned chicken, brown it before placing it on the rice.

CHEDDAR CHICKEN

ingredients

- 1 (10 oz.) frozen chopped broccoli
- 2 whole chicken breasts
- 4 tbsp. butter
- 1/2 lb. shredded mild cheddar cheese
- 1/3 c. milk
- 2 tbsp. sliced almonds

directions

1. Place chopped broccoli in 8x12" baking dish. Set aside to thaw.
2. Cut chicken in cubes

CHICKEN SPECTACULAR

ingredients

- 3 c.
- Cooked chicken
- 1 pkg. Uncle Ben's Wild White Rice, cooked
- 1 can cream of celery soup
- 1 med. onion, chopped
- 2 c. French style green beans, drained
- 1 c. Hellmann's mayonnaise
- 1 c. water chestnuts, diced
- 1 med. jar sliced pimientos (for color, if desired)

directions

1. Mix all ingredients.
2. Pour into a 2 1/2 or 3-quart casserole.
3. Bake at 350 degrees for 25 to 30 minutes.

CHICKEN & RICE CASSEROLE

ingredients

- 1 c. uncooked rice
- 1 can cream of chicken soup
- 1 pkg. Good Season Italian dressing mix
- 2 c. boiling water
- 2 1/2-3 lb.
- Cut up chicken or chicken breasts

directions

1. Wash and drain the rice. Spread in 9 x 13-inch baking dish or 3-quart casserole.
2. Combine soup, Italian dressing mix, and water.
3. Add the rice, salt and pepper, and chicken pieces. Place the skin side up over the rice mixture.
4. Cover tightly with foil and cook for 1 hour at 350 degrees. Uncover and cook for 20 more minutes to dry the rice.
5. Place the casserole under the broiler for a few seconds to brown the chicken. Serves 6-8.
6. * Cream of mushrooms can be substituted for cream of chicken.

PARMESAN CHICKEN

ingredients

- 1 c. crushed Ritz crackers
- 3/4 c. Parmesan cheese
- 4 boneless chicken breasts
- 1/4 c.
- Melted margarine

directions

1. Mix 3/4 cup of Parmesan cheese with each 1 cup of crushed Ritz cracker crumbs.
2. Dip the boneless chicken breasts in melted margarine then roll in the crumb mixture. Next, roll the chicken breast from wide end to narrow end. Place in a baking dish seam side down.
3. Bake at 350 degrees for 1 hour.
4. Cover the first 1/2 hour of cooking and then remove the lid for the last 1/2 hour. Increase recipe according to needs.

CHICKEN POT PIE

ingredients

- 2 c. chicken (1 fryer or 4 breasts)
- 1 (20 oz.) pkg. frozen mixed vegetables
- 2 cans cream of chicken soup
- 1 c. chicken broth
- TOPPING
- 1 c. self rising flour
- 1 stick margarine
- 1 c. milk

directions

1. Cut the chicken into chunks. It can be precooked. For convenience, canned chicken breast can be used. Place the vegetable, chicken, and soup mixture in a greased 2-quart casserole.
2. Pour topping over batter and bake at 400 degrees for 1 hour or until golden brown.

CHICKEN CASSEROLE

ingredients

- 1/3 c. margarine
- 1/3 c. flour
- 1 c. broth
- 1 c. milk
- Salt & pepper to taste
- 1 tbsp. chopped onion
- 3 c.
- Cut up chicken
- 1 can whole kernel corn
- 3/4 c. grated sharp cheese
- 1/4 c. pimiento

directions

1. Make white sauce (first 6 ingredients).
2. Mix all the ingredients and put in a saucepan.
3. Top with buttered breadcrumbs and bake at 350 degrees until bubbly.

CHICKEN CASSEROLE

ingredients

- 1 fryer or chicken breast (stewed)
- 2 cans cream of chicken soup
- 1 pkg. Pepperidge Farm dressing mix
- 1 c. chicken broth
- 1 c. milk

directions

1. Remove the skin and bone from the stewed chicken.
2. Place in bottom of 13x9 "baking dish.
3. Top with chicken soup. Prepare dressing as directed on package. Place over the chicken on a plate.

CHICKEN BENGALI

ingredients

- 1 tbsp. margarine
- 1 1/2 tsp. flour
- 1 1/2 tsp. Worcestershire sauce
- 1 tsp. powder mustard
- 1/2 tsp. curry powder
- 1 1/2 lbs. chicken thighs, skinned

directions

1. Preheat the oven to 375 degrees. In a small saucepan, heat the margarine over medium heat until bubbly and hot.
2. Add remaining ingredients except chicken until mixture is smooth.
3. Place in 9x9 "baking dish sprinkled with Pam. Arrange the chicken in individual layers.
4. Bake until chicken is golden.

ITALIAN CHICKEN CUTLETS

ingredients

- 2 whole chicken breasts, skinned, boned, halved
- 1/4 c. flour
- 3/4 c. dry bread crumbs
- 1 tsp. dried oregano leaves
- 1/4 tsp. salt
- 1 egg, beaten
- 1 tbsp. water
- 1 (8 oz.) can tomato sauce
- 1/4 tsp. dried basil leaves
- 1/8 tsp. garlic powder
- 1/4 c. oil
- 4 slices (4 oz.) Mozzarella cheese
- 1/4 c. grated Parmesan cheese

directions

1. Place 1 chicken breast half, boneless side up, between 2 pieces of plastic wrap or wax paper. Working from the center, gently pat the chicken with a rolling pin or the flat side of the meat mallet until it is about 1/4-inch thick. Repeat with the rest of the chicken pieces, forming 4 cutlets. Coat the chicken cutlets with flour.
2. On a flat plate, combine the breadcrumbs, oregano, and salt. In another shallow dish, combine the egg and water.
3. Dip each cutlet in egg mixture; top with crumb mixture. In a small saucepan, combine the tomato sauce, basil, and garlic powder.
4. Cook over low heat until heated through, stirring occasionally. Meanwhile, heat oil in large skillet over medium high heat until wavy.
5. Add the chops; cook until crisp and golden on one side, 6 to 8 minutes. Turn; cook other side about 2 minutes or until chicken is no longer pink.
6. Top each cutlet with a slice of cheese.
7. Cover skillet to melt cheese, about 1 minute.
8. Place the chop on a serving plate. Serve with sauce and Parmesan cheese. 4 portions.

NO PEEK CHICKEN

ingredients

- 1 1/2 c. Minute Rice, uncooked
- 1 chicken, cut up or pieces
- 1 pkg. dry onion soup mix
- 1 can cream of mushroom soup
- 1 can cream of celery soup

directions

1. Mix the dry rice with the mushroom and celery soup. Rinse the cans with a little water and add to mix.
2. Place the chicken on top of the rice mixture.
3. Sprinkle onion soup over chicken rice mixture. Seal the pan completely with aluminum foil.
4. Bake at 325 degrees for 1 hour. Do not look or uncover until ready.

SUNDAY DINNER CHICKEN

ingredients

- 8 chicken breasts (boneless and skinless)
- 1 pkg. chipped beef or 1 jar smoked chipped beef
- 1 can undiluted cream of chicken soup
- 1/2 pt. sour cream
- (if desired - wrap each piece of chicken with 1 piece of bacon)

directions

1. Line the bottom of a greased, flat baking dish (8x12) with minced meat. Place the chicken on top of the meat.
2. Mix the soup and sour cream.
3. Pour over the chicken.
4. Bake at 275 degrees for 3 hours uncovered. Makes 8 servings.
5. Put in the oven when you go out for Sunday school and church.
6. When you get home, cook the veggies, make the salad, and dinner is on the table in 20 minutes.

SKILLET BARBECUED CHICKEN

ingredients

- Chicken, with or without skin, bone or boneless
- 2 tbsp. butter
- 1 tsp. curry powder
- 1 clove garlic, minced
- 1 can onion soup
- 2 tbsp. flour
- 1 1/2 c. of water
- 1/2 c. of ketchup
- 1 tbsp. honey
- 1 tsp. Worcestershire sauce

directions

1. In a large skillet, melt the butter with the curry powder and garlic.
2. Add the chicken and brown.
3. Remove the chicken. In the fat, mix the soup and flour. Gradually add the remaining ingredients. Return the chicken to the skillet.
4. Cover and simmer until chicken is cooked. Approximately 1 hour. Serve with rice or noodles.

HOT CHICKEN SALAD

ingredients

- 4 c. diced chicken (6 breasts, baked)
- 2 c. diced celery
- 1/3 c. mayonnaise
- 1 can cream of mushroom soup
- 1 sm. jar chopped pimiento
- 1 can sliced water chestnuts, drained
- 1 tsp. salt
- 1 tsp. chopped onion
- 3 tsp. lemon juice
- 1 c. grated cheese
- 1 c. crushed potato chips
- 1/2 c. slivered almonds

directions

1. Blend the first nine ingredients and pour into a 9x13" pan.
2. Top with the grated cheese

LIGHT CAPITAL CHICKEN

ingredients

- 2 tbsp. corn oil margarine
- 4 tbsp. flour
- 3/4 c. defatted chicken stock
- 1/2 c. skim milk
- 1 tbsp. canola oil
- 3 whole chicken breasts, boned, skinned, split, about
- 1 1/2 lbs. total
- 8 oz. fresh mushrooms, sliced, about 3 cups
- 1 c. each, dry white wine, water
- 1/2 c. 2% milk
- 3/4 tsp. salt
- 1/4 tsp. dried tarragon leaves, crushed Dash garlic powder
- 1/4 tsp. freshly ground black pepper
- 2 tbsp. each, chopped green onions, fresh parsley

directions

1. Heat the oven to 350 degrees.
2. Melt 1 tablespoon of margarine in a medium saucepan.
3. Add 3 tablespoons of flour and stir over medium heat for 1 minute; do not brown.
4. Add the chicken broth and skim milk. Using a wire whisk, stir mixture over medium heat until boiling.
5. Continue cooking 1 minute more; set aside.
6. Melt remaining
7. 1 tablespoon margarine in a large skillet along with canola oil.
8. Add the chicken and cook over medium heat until golden brown on both sides, about 5 minutes.
9. Remove the chicken and place in a baking dish sprayed with a nonstick vegetable coating.
10. Cook the mushrooms in the same skillet for 5 minutes.
11. Add the remaining tablespoon of flour, sauce, wine, and water. Cook over low heat, stirring, until thickened about 10 minutes.
12. Add the 2% milk, salt, tarragon, garlic powder, and pepper.
13. Pour over chicken and bake uncovered until hot (45 minutes).
14. Sprinkle with green onions and parsley; bake 5 minutes.

CHICKEN A LA KING

ingredients

- 2 tablespoons fat
- 2 tablespoons flour
- 1 cup milk
- 1 cup cream
- 2 egg yolks
- 1 green pepper, minced
- 1 cup quartered mushrooms
- 1 pimiento cut in narrow strips
- 2 cups cooked diced chicken
- 1 teaspoon salt
- 1/2 teaspoon pepper

directions

1. Make a white sauce with meat fat, flour, milk, cream, salt and pepper.
2. Add the mushrooms, green bell pepper, bell pepper, and chicken.
3. Cook until the meat is done. Just before serving, add the egg yolks, lightly beaten, and cook for a minute or two, stirring constantly. Serve immediately on hot toast.

TERIYAKI CHICKEN

ingredients

- 1 chicken, cut up or 2 lbs.
- Teriyaki beef or top sirloin steak sliced thin 2 tsp.
- grated fresh ginger
- 1 clove garlic,
- chopped fine 1 medium onion,
- chopped 1/3 c. soy sauce
- 1/4 c. sugar
- 1/4 c. sake
- TERIYAKI MARINADE
- 1 c. soy sauce
- 1 1/2 - 1 1/4 c.
- Brown sugar
- 1 tsp. oyster sauce
- 1 tsp. mirin (sweet rice wine)
- 1 clove chopped garlic Grated fresh ginger

directions

1. Mix all the ingredients except the meat.
2. Stir and simmer until the sugar dissolves. Cool.
3. Pour over the meat and marinate for at least 1 hour. Best when cooked over charcoal. Use the remaining marinade for basting. If using Quick Teriyaki marinade, mix and marinate the meat for about 1/2 hour. Better when the meat is cooked over charcoal. Baste often.

TARRAGON CHICKEN

ingredients

- 2 whole chicken breasts, boned skinned and pounded to 1/4 inch thickness All purpose flour
- 4 tbsp. butter, divided
- 1/2 lb. sliced mushrooms
- 2 tbsp. all purpose flour
- 1 c. chicken broth
- 1 1/4 tsp. minced fresh tarragon or 1/4 tsp. dried tarragon
- 1/2 c. half and half
- Salt and freshly ground black pepper to taste

directions

1. Drain the chicken breasts in flour and brown in 2 tablespoons of butter.
2. Remove the chicken to a hot plate.
3. Add the remaining 2 tablespoons of butter and sauté the mushrooms.
4. Sprinkle the mushrooms with 2 tablespoons of flour, mix well. Gradually add chicken broth, then tarragon, cook until thickened. Slowly add half and half, and season with salt and pepper. Return the chicken to the skillet and heat. The sauce should be slightly thick.

CHICKEN SPAGHETTI

ingredients

- 1 whole chicken, cooked & boned
- 1 can Rotel tomatoes
- 1 lb. Velveeta cheese Spaghetti
- 1 onion
- 1 bell pepper

directions

1. Sauté the onion and bell pepper in butter.
2. Add the cheese (cubed) and let it melt.
3. Add can of Rotel.
4. Cook the spaghetti, drain and mix all the ingredients.

EASY CHICKEN POT PIE

ingredients

- 2 c. diced, cooked chicken
- 1 med. onion, chopped
- 4 boiled eggs, grated or chopped
- 2 cans mixed vegetables, drained
- 2 cans cream of chicken soup
- 1 can cream of celery soup
- 1/2 c. chicken broth
- CRUST
- 1 c. sweet milk 1 c. mayonnaise
- 1 c. self-rising flour

directions

1. Layer the first three ingredients on the plate.
2. Mix soup, broths, and vegetables.
3. Pour over the chicken.
4. Mix the milk, mayonnaise and flour; Spread over soup mix to form base.
5. Bake at 350 degrees for 1 to 1 1/2 hours until golden brown.

CHEESY PARSLEY CHICKEN

ingredients

- 1 clove crushed garlic 1/4 lb. butter, melted
- 1 C. dried bread crumbs
- 1/3 C. grated Parmesan cheese 2 tbsp chopped fresh parsley 1 tsp salt
- 1/8 tsp ground black pepper
- 1 (4 lb.) chicken, cut into pieces

directions

1. Set your oven to 350 degrees F before doing anything else and grease a 13x9-inch baking dish. In a shallow dish, combine the melted butter and garlic.
2. In another shallow dish, mix the cheese, breadcrumbs, parsley, salt, and black pepper.
3. Coat the chicken pieces in the butter mixture and cheese mixture evenly.
4. Place chicken pieces in prepared baking dish in a single layer.
5. Drizzle evenly with the remaining butter mixture and cook everything in the oven for about 1-1 1/4 hours.

CHICKEN DELIGHT

ingredients

- 15-20 cut up chicken pieces
- 1 can cream of chicken soup
- 1 can cream of celery soup
- 1 green bell pepper
- 1 red or yellow pepper
- 1 can water

directions

1. Wash the chicken. Season with pepper and your favorite seasoning salt. (I like McCormick's.) Refrigerate the chicken overnight so the seasonings are completely soaked.
2. Cut the peppers into slices and reserve.
3. Mix the soups and water in a bowl.
4. Add the bell peppers and pour over the chicken.
5. Bake at 350 degrees for about 1 hour and 15 minutes.
6. NOTE: The broth in this dish can be used as a dressing sauce.

CRISPY PAPRIKA CHICKEN

ingredients

- 1 (4 lb.) chicken, cut into pieces
- 1 C. buttermilk
- 2 C. all-purpose flour for coating
- 1 tsp paprika
- salt and pepper to taste
- 2 quarts vegetable oil for frying

directions

1. On a shallow plate, place the buttermilk.
2. In another flat plate, place the flour, salt, black pepper and paprika.
3. Completely submerge the chicken pieces in the buttermilk and coat with the flour mixture.
4. Place the chicken pieces in a baking dish and cover with wax paper and set aside until the flour turns mushy.
5. In a large cast iron skillet, heat the vegetable oil and fry the chicken pieces until golden brown.
6. Reduce heat and cook covered for about 30 minutes.
7. Uncover and increase heat and cook until crisp.
8. Transfer chicken pieces to plates lined with paper towels to drain.

CHICKEN STEAKS WITH GRAVY

ingredients

- 4 (1/2 lb.) chicken cube steaks 2 C. all-purpose flour
- 2 tsp baking powder 1 tsp baking soda
- 1 tsp black pepper 3/4 tsp salt
- 1 1/2 C. buttermilk 1 egg
- 1 tbsp hot pepper sauce 2 cloves garlic, minced
- 3 C. vegetable shortening for deep frying
- 1/4 C. all-purpose flour 4 C. milk
- kosher salt and ground black pepper to taste

directions

1. Using a meat grinder, mash the steaks until they are 1/4-inch thick.
2. In a shallow dish, mix together the flour, baking soda, baking powder, salt, and black pepper.
3. In another shallow dish, add the egg, buttermilk, hot sauce, and garlic and beat well.
4. Coat the steaks with the flour mixture, then dip them in the egg mixture and cover with the flour mixture again.
5. In a large skillet, heat the oil to 325 degrees F.
6. Add the fillets and fry for about 3-5 minutes on both sides.
7. Transfer the steaks to plates lined with paper towels to drain.
8. Drain the fat from the skillet, reserving about 1/4 C. of the mixture in the skillet.
9. Gradually add the remaining flour, stirring continuously in the skillet over medium-low heat.
10. Gradually add the milk, stirring continuously, and increase the heat to medium.
11. Bring to a simmer and cook for about 6-7 minutes.
12. Add the salt and black pepper and remove from the heat.
13. Pour sauce over chicken and serve.

CRISPY CHICKEN

ingredients

- 2 tsp garlic powder
- 1 tsp ground black pepper
- 1 tsp salt
- 1 tsp paprika
- 1/2 C. seasoned bread crumbs
- 1 C. all-purpose flour
- 1/2 C. milk
- 1 egg
- 4 skinless, boneless chicken breast halves
- 1 C. oil for frying, or as needed

directions

1. In a shallow dish, add the egg and milk and beat well.
2. In another shallow dish mix the flour, bread-crumbs, garlic powder, paprika, salt, and black pepper.
3. Put your oil in a pan set at 350 degrees F.
4. Dip the chicken breast halves into the egg mix-ture then roll the flour mixture evenly.
5. Fry the chicken breast halves for about 10 min-utes, turning once in half.
6. Serve hot.

INDIAN STYLE FRIED CHICKEN

ingredients

- 1 (4 lb.) whole chicken, cut into pieces
- 6 cloves garlic, chopped 4 tbsp oyster sauce
- 2 tbsp curry powder 1/2 C. vegetable oil

directions

1. In a glass dish, combine the oyster sauce, garlic, and curry powder.
2. Add the chicken pieces and generously coat with the mixture.
3. Cover and refrigerate for at least 1/2 hour.
4. In a large skillet, heat the oil over medium-high heat and fry the chicken pieces for about 20-25 minutes.

SWEET GARLICKY CRISPY CHICKEN

ingredients

- 4 eggs
- 1/4 C. cornstarch
- 1/4 C. white sugar
- 5 cloves garlic, minced
- 1/2 C. sweet rice flour
- 4 tsp salt
- 4 green onions, chopped
- 1/4 C. oyster sauce
- 5 lb. boneless chicken thighs, cut in half
- 2 C. vegetable oil, for deep frying

directions

1. In a large bowl, combine all ingredients except chicken and oil.
2. Add the chicken pieces and cover generously with the mixture.
3. Cover and refrigerate everything to marinate overnight.
4. Remove the chicken pieces from the refrigerator and set everything aside at room temperature for about 10 minutes before cooking.
5. In a large skillet, heat the oil to 375 degrees F and fry the chicken pieces until completely browned.
6. Transfer chicken pieces to plates lined with paper towels to drain.

CRISPY CHICKEN CROQUETTES

ingredients

- 1/4 C. butter
- 1/4 C. flour
- 1/2 C. milk
- 1/2 C. chicken broth
- 3 C. finely chopped cooked chicken
- 1 1/2 C. seasoned bread crumbs, divided
- 2 eggs, beaten
- 1/4 C. minced onion
- 1 tbsp dried parsley
- 1/4 tsp garlic powder
- 1/8 tsp celery seed
- 1/8 tsp cayenne pepper
- salt and ground black pepper to taste
- 1/4 C. oil, or as needed

directions

1. In a skillet, melt the butter over medium heat.
2. Gradually add the flour, stirring continuously, and cook for about 1 minute.
3. Gradually add the broth and milk, whisking continuously.
4. Cook, stirring continuously for about 5-10 minutes until a thick sauce forms.
5. Remove everything from the heat and let it rest for about 10 minutes to cool.
6. In a large bowl, add the cooled sauce, chicken, eggs, 1 cup breadcrumbs, onion, parsley, celery seeds, garlic powder, salt, and black pepper and mix until just fine. combined.
7. Cover and refrigerate to marinate for about 2 hours.
8. Make 6 patties of equal size with the mixture.
9. In a shallow dish, place the remaining breadcrumbs.
10. Roll each burger in the breadcrumbs.
11. In a large skillet, heat the oil over medium-high heat and cook the patties for about 5 minutes per side. Transfer chicken to plates lined with paper towels to drain.

HONEY COATED CHICKEN

ingredients

- 3 C. cold water
- 1/4 C. kosher salt
- 1/4 C. honey
- 4 boneless skinless chicken breast halves
- 1/4 C. buttermilk
- 1 C. all-purpose flour
- 1 tsp black pepper
- 1/2 tsp garlic salt
- 1/2 tsp onion salt cayenne pepper to taste vegetable oil for frying

directions

1. In a large bowl, add the water, honey, and salt and mix until the honey dissolves.
2. Add the chicken breast halves and top with the honey mixture generously and place a heavy plate over the chicken to completely submerge it.
3. Cover and refrigerate everything to marinate for about 1 hour.
4. Remove the chicken breast halves from the marinade and pat dry with a paper towel and transfer the meat to a bowl.
5. Add the buttermilk and set it aside for about 15 minutes.
6. On a shallow plate, place the flour, onion salt, garlic salt, cayenne pepper, salt, and black pepper.
7. Coat the chicken breast halves with the flour mixture evenly and place everything on a wire rack for about 15 minutes.
8. In a large skillet, heat the oil to 350 degrees F and fry the chicken breast halves for about 15-20 minutes.
9. Transfer chicken to plates lined with paper towels to drain.

CHICKEN & VEGETABLES WITH RICE

ingredients

- 2 C. white rice
- 4 C. water
- 2/3 C. soy sauce
- 1/4 C.
- Brown sugar
- 1 tbsp cornstarch
- 1 tbsp minced fresh ginger
- 1 tbsp minced garlic
- 1/4 tsp red pepper flakes
- 3 skinless, boneless chicken breast halves, thinly sliced
- 1 tbsp sesame oil
- 1 green bell pepper, cut into matchsticks
- 1 (8 oz.) can sliced water chestnuts, drained
- 1 head broccoli, broken into florets
- 1 C. sliced carrots
- 1 onion, cut into large chunks
- 1 tbsp sesame oil

directions

1. In a skillet, add the water and rice and bring to a boil over high heat.
2. Reduce heat to medium-low and simmer, covered for about 20-25 minutes.
3. In a small bowl, add the brown sugar, cornstarch, and soy sauce and mix until smooth.
4. Add the garlic, ginger, and red pepper flakes and mix well.
5. Add the chicken slices and coat everything with the mixture generously.
6. Cover and refrigerate to marinate for about 15-20 minutes.
7. In a large skillet, heat 1 tablespoon of the oil over medium-high heat and sauté the vegetables for about 5 minutes. Transfer vegetables to a large plate and cover with foil to keep warm.
8. In the same skillet, heat the remaining oil over medium-high heat.
9. Remove the chicken slices from the refrigerator and place the chicken in the skillet, reserving the marinade.
10. Sauté the chicken for about 2 minutes per side.
11. Add reserved marinade and vegetable mixture and bring to a boil.
12. Cook, stirring occasionally, for about 5-7 minutes.
13. Serve the chicken mixture over the rice.

SPICY CHICKEN WINGS

ingredients

- 12 small chicken wings
- 1/4 tsp seasoned salt, or to taste
- 1 C. all-purpose flour
- 1 tsp coarse salt
- 1/2 tsp ground black pepper
- 1/4 tsp cayenne pepper
- 1/4 tsp paprika
- 1 (12 fluid oz.) bottle Buffalo wing sauce
- 2 quarts vegetable oil for frying

directions

1. Sprinkle the chicken wings with the seasoned salt evenly.
2. On a shallow plate, combine the flour, paprika, cayenne pepper, salt, and black pepper.
3. Cover and refrigerate to marinate for about 15-30 minutes.
4. In a large skillet, heat the oil to 375 degrees F and fry the chicken wings for about 10 minutes on both sides. Transfer chicken to plates lined with paper towels to drain.

CHICKEN WITH MULTI-GRAIN & VEGGIES

ingredients

- 1 bag Multi-Grain Medley, uncooked
- 1 C. chicken broth
- 2 large eggs, lightly beaten
- 1/2 tsp sesame oil
- 2 tbsp olive oil, divided
- 2 cloves garlic, chopped
- 1/2 C. red onion, thinly sliced
- 1/2 C. snap peas
- 1/2 C. broccoli florets
- 1/2 C. red bell pepper, sliced
- 1/2 tsp Chinese five-spice powder
- 2 C.
- Cooked chicken, shredded

directions

1. Cook Multi-Grain with its broth according to package directions.
2. In a small bowl, add the sesame oil and eggs and beat well.
3. In a large skillet, heat 1/2 tablespoon of the oil over medium-low heat.
4. Add the egg mixture and cook until scrambled and transfer to a bowl.
5. Cover the scrambled eggs with aluminum foil to keep them warm.
6. In the same skillet, heat the remaining oil and sauté the remaining ingredients, except the chicken, for about 3 minutes.
7. Add the scrambled eggs, Multigrain, and chicken and sauté for about 2 minutes.

CHICKEN WITH SPINACH &RICE

ingredients

- Ingredients
- 1 C.
- Brown rice
- 2 C. water
- 1 tbsp olive oil
- 4 skinless, boneless chicken breast halves,
- 1/2-inch thick
- coarse salt to taste
- 2 tbsp olive oil
- 2 cloves garlic, chopped
- 1 pinch red pepper flakes
- 1 bunch fresh spinach leaves, trimmed and rinsed
- 2 tbsp pine nuts
- 2 tbsp crumbled goat cheese
- 1/2 lemon, juiced

directions

1. In a skillet, add the water and brown rice and bring to a boil.
2. Reduce heat to medium-low and simmer, covered for about 45-50 minutes.
3. Meanwhile, in a large skillet, heat 1 tablespoon of the oil over medium heat.
4. Season the chicken with the salt and sauté everything in the hot oil for about 5-8 minutes on both sides.
5. Transfer the chicken to a plate. In the same skillet, heat the remaining oil and sauté the garlic and red pepper flakes for about 1 minute.
6. Add the spinach and cook for about 2 minutes.
7. Divide rice among serving plates and top with chicken breasts and spinach evenly.
8. Sprinkle everything with the pine nuts and goat cheese and serve with a splash of lemon juice.

FRIED CHICKEN & RICE

ingredients

- 3 tbsp oyster sauce
- 2 tbsp fish sauce
- 1 tsp white sugar
- 1/2 C. peanut oil for frying
- 4 C.
- Cooked jasmine rice, chilled
- 6 large cloves garlic clove, crushed
- 2 serrano peppers, crushed
- 1 lb. boneless, skinless chicken breast, cut into thin strips
- 1 red pepper, seeded and thinly sliced
- 1 onion, thinly sliced
- 2 C. sweet Thai basil
- 1 cucumber, sliced
- 1/2 C. cilantro sprigs

directions

1. In a bowl, add the fish sauce, oyster sauce, and sugar and beat until well combined.
2. In a large skillet, heat the oil over medium-high heat and sauté the serrano pepper and garlic for a while.
3. Add the chicken strips, sugar mixture, onion and bell pepper and sauté until the chicken is golden brown.
4. Increase the heat to high and add the rice and sauté until the rice is mixed with the chicken mixture.
5. Add the basil and immediately remove everything from the heat. Serve with a cucumber and coriander garnish.

FLOUR COATED CHICKEN LIVERS

ingredients

- 1 lb. chicken livers
- 1 egg
- 1/2 C. milk
- 1 C. all-purpose flour
- 1 tbsp garlic powder salt and pepper to taste
- 1 quart vegetable oil for frying

directions

1. In a colander, rinse the chicken livers and set aside to drain completely.
2. In a shallow dish, add the milk and egg and beat well.
3. In another shallow plate, place the flour, salt, black pepper, and garlic powder.
4. Dip the chicken livers into the milk mixture and then coat with the flour mixture evenly.
5. In a large skillet, heat the oil to 375 degrees F and fry the chicken livers for about 5-6 minutes.
6. Transfer chicken livers to plates lined with paper towels to drain.

POTATO FLAKES COATED CHICKEN

ingredients

- 1 (3 lb.) whole chicken, cut into pieces
- 2 C. buttermilk
- 1 C. dry potato flakes
- 1 C. all-purpose flour
- 1 tsp poultry seasoning
- 1/2 tsp salt
- 1 tsp freshly ground black pepper
- 2 C. vegetable oil for frying

directions

1. In a shallow dish, mix together the chicken pieces and buttermilk.
2. Cover and refrigerate to marinate overnight.
3. In another shallow dish, mix all the remaining ingredients.
4. Remove the chicken pieces from the buttermilk and coat with the flour mixture evenly and set aside for about 15 minutes.
5. In a large skillet, heat the oil to 350 degrees F and fry the chicken pieces until completely browned.
6. Transfer chicken to plates lined with paper towels to drain.

CHICKEN TENDERLOINS WITH CREAMY DIPPING SAUCE

ingredients

- 1 C. all-purpose flour
- 2 C. Italian-style seasoned bread crumbs
- 1/2 tsp ground black pepper
- 1/2 tsp cayenne pepper
- 2 eggs, beaten
- 2 tbsp water
- 24 chicken tenderloins
- 2 quarts oil for frying
- 1 C. mayonnaise
- 3 tbsp prepared horseradish
- 1/2 C. sour cream
- 1 dash Worcestershire sauce
- 3 tbsp prepared mustard

directions

1. On a shallow plate, place the flour. In a second shallow dish, whisk together the water and eggs.
2. In a third shallow dish, mix together the breadcrumbs, cayenne pepper, and black pepper.
3. First coat the chicken fillets with the flour, followed by the egg mixture and the breadcrumbs. In a large skillet, heat the oil to 375 degrees F and fry the chicken fillets for about 6-8 minutes. Meanwhile, for the sauce, in a bowl, mix the remaining ingredients.
4. Transfer chicken to plates lined with paper towels to drain.
5. Serve the chicken with the dipping sauce.

SWEET & SPICY GARLICKY CHICKEN

ingredients

- 8 skinless, boneless chicken breast
- halves, pounded to 3/4-inch thickness
- 1 quart buttermilk
- 3 shallots, finely chopped
- 2 tbsp chopped garlic
- 2 tbsp salt
- 2 tbsp white sugar
- 1 1/4 tsp ground cumin
- 1 1/2 tsp ground black pepper
- 2 C. vegetable oil for frying
- 4 C. all-purpose flour
- 2 tbsp baking powder
- 2 tsp salt
- 8 large eggs, beaten

directions

1. In a resealable bag, combine the buttermilk, garlic, shallots, sugar, cumin, salt, and black pepper.
2. Add chicken breast halves and seal bag tightly and shake to coat well.
3. Refrigerate to marinate overnight. In a shallow dish, mix together the flour, baking powder, and salt.
4. In another shallow dish, add the eggs.
5. Remove the chicken breast halves from the refrigerator and shake off excess marinade.
6. First, coat the chicken breast halves with the flour mixture, then dip everything in the eggs and again cover with the flour mixture.
7. In a large skillet, heat the oil over medium heat and fry the chicken breasts in halves for about 2-3 minutes per side.
8. Transfer chicken to plates lined with paper towels to drain.

SPICE COATED CHICKEN

ingredients

- Ingredients
- 2 C. oil
- 1 C. gluten-free all-purpose flour
- 2 tsp powdered buttermilk
- 1 tsp paprika
- 1 tsp celery salt
- 1/2 tsp ground white pepper
- 1/2 tsp xanthan gum
- 1/2 tsp baking soda
- 1/4 tsp cayenne pepper
- 2 lb. skinless, boneless chicken breast halves

directions

1. In a large, shallow dish, mix all ingredients except chicken breast halves and oil.
2. Add the chicken breast halves and generously coat with the mixture.
3. In a large skillet, heat the oil to 375 degrees F and fry the chicken fillets for about 5 minutes per side.
4. Transfer chicken to plates lined with paper towels to drain.

TOMATO SOUP & SALAD DRESSING COATED CHICKEN

ingredients

- 2 eggs, beaten
- 2/3 C. milk
- 1 1/2 C. all-purpose flour
- 1 (.7 oz.) package dry Italian-style salad dressing mix
- 1 packet dry tomato soup mix
- 1 (4 lb.) whole chicken, cut into pieces
- 2 tbsp vegetable oil

directions

1. In a shallow dish, beat the eggs and milk.
2. In another plate, mix the remaining ingredients except the chicken and oil.
3. Dip the chicken pieces in the egg mixture and roll them in the flour mixture evenly.
4. In a large skillet, heat the oil over medium-high heat and fry the chicken pieces for about 25-35 minutes, turning occasionally.
5. Transfer chicken to plates lined with paper towels to drain.

Anatomy of the Chicken

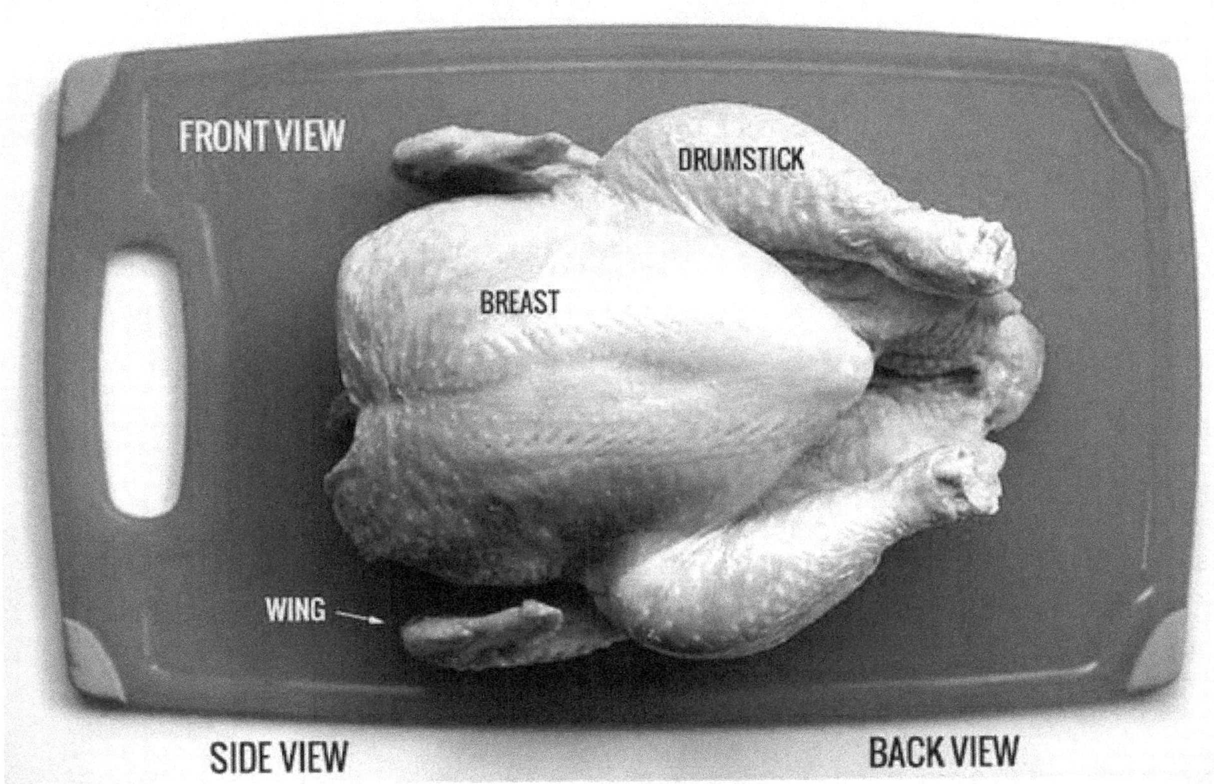

SIDE VIEW

BACK VIEW

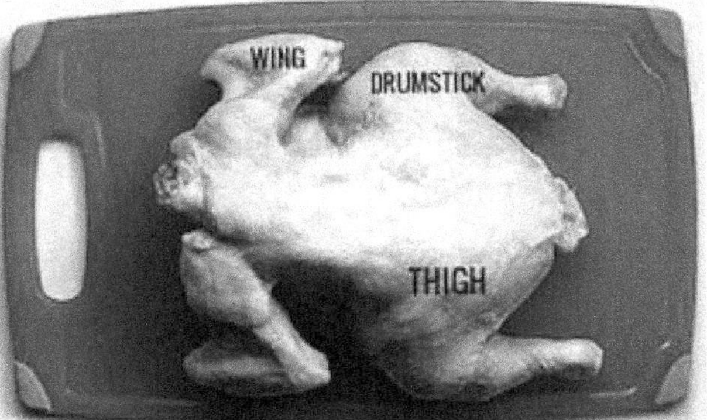

ANATOMY OF THE CHICKEN

Head

The head is the talkie part of South Africa's famous walkie-talkies and stewing and braising are the best ways to cook it.

Breast

This very lean cut is best cooked quickly to keep them moist, for instance grilling, frying and braaiing. When stewing for braising breasts, don't overcook them as they will become dry and stringy.

Wing

Wings are high in fat and can withstand heat without becoming dry. They therefore are suited to deep- frying, braaiing and roasting. But however you cook them,

Tail

TAILS The tail is often attached to the thigh. It is packed with flavour because it contains a lot of fat and, thanks to the large skin area, becomes very crispy.

ANATOMY OF THE CHICKEN

Neck

This bony cut has very little meat but is an inexpensive way to flavour sauces and stock.

Thighs

Like drumsticks, thighs will be rather tough if not cooked properly. They have loads of fantastic flavour and are best when roasted or braised slowly or added to stews.

Drumstic

This popular cut could also be tough if it hasn't been cooked for long enough. The delicious dark brown meat particularly takes time and drumsticks taste best when they've been roasted, stewed, braised or braaied.

Feet

The other half of walkie-talkies, chicken feet are bony and low on meat. Once cooked, though, they are tender and can be eaten whole. Braai or grill them if you like crisp, crunchy skin.

HOW MANY CALORIES IN CHICKEN?

Chicken tenders

263 calories per 3.5 ounces (100 grams)

Back

137 calories per 3.5 ounces (100 grams)

Dark meat

125 calories per 3.5 ounces (100 grams)

Light meat

114 calories per 3.5 ounces (100 grams)

HOW MANY CALORIES IN CHICKEN?

Breast

A 3.5-ounce (100-gram) serving of chicken breast provides 165 calories, 31 grams of protein and 3.6 grams of fat.

Thigh

A 3.5-ounce (100-gram) serving of chicken thigh provides 209 calories, 26 grams of protein and 10.9 grams of fat.

Wing

Per 3.5 ounces (100 grams), chicken wings provide 203 calories, 30.5 grams of protein and 8.1 grams of fat.

Drumstick

Per 3.5 ounces (100 grams), chicken drumsticks have 172 calories, 28.3 grams of protein and 5.7 grams of fat.

Skin

While a skinless chicken breast is 284 calories with 80% protein and 20% fat, those numbers **dramatically** shift when you include the skin. One boneless, cooked chicken breast with skin (196 grams) contains: Calories: 386, Protein: 58.4 grams, Fat: 15.2 grams

COOKING METHODS

Grilling

This is one of the more common cooking methods, as it tends to require less added fat.

Baking or roasting

These other common methods are sufficient when you don't have access to a grill.

Broiling

This is similar to grilling, but you usually do it in a standard oven or toaster oven.

Braising

Lightly panfry the chicken and then cook it covered, submerged in liquid, for an extended time at a lower temperature.

COOKING METHODS

Fried

The chicken is submerged in hot cooking oil in either a pan or deep fryer. This creates a crisp outer coating but adds quite a bit of fat.

Baking or roasting

These other common methods are sufficient when you don't have access to a grill.

Boiling

You submerge the meat in boiling water and cook it until the internal temperature reaches 165°F (74°C). This is the leanest method, as it doesn't require added fats. Still, some may find the texture lacking.

Quick Recipes

Lemon Garlic Chicken

Place whole roasting chicken in baker with one whole lemon and one head of garlic (unpeeled) in cavity of chicken. Season with salt and pepper. Cover with lid and cook for 1-1/2 hours at 425°. (Try with an orange too.)

Roasted Turkey Breast

Place turkey breast in baker; place 6-8 small red skinned potatoes, halved, around turkey. Add 1/2 cup white wine and 2 cloves pressed garlic. Season with salt and pepper. Cover with lid. Bake at 350°F for 1-1/2 hours. Uncover for last 15-20 minutes. Let stand 5 minutes before slicing.

Honey Mustard Chicken

Place roasting chicken in the baker and pour fat free honey mustard dressing over the top. Cover with lid. Roast for 1-1/2 hours at 425°F.

3 CHEFS' TIPS
A little know-how can make life in the kitchen a lot easier

Done Yet

There are two ways to check if a chicken breast is done.
The first is to insert the tip of a small knife into the thickest part of the meat. If the juices are clear, it is cooked; if it's still pink,
you need to cook longer. Alternatively, make a small incision in the thickest part of the breast. If the meat is completely white and you don't see any pink meat, the brisket is done. The juices will also be clear. This method also works for testing whole chickens and other chicken pieces.

Slicing chicken breast for stir fry

Place the chicken breast, smooth-side down on a cutting board.
Cut it diagonally into 1 cm strips and halve each strip lengthwise into longer, thinner strips before cutting them diagonally across the fibres to keep it tender.

Butterflying chicken breasts for schnitzels

Place the chicken breast smooth side down on a cutting board. Make a shallow incision along one side and continue as if you were trying to cut the breast into two identical halves. Stop just before cutting it all the way so the top and bottom half open like a book. With a meat mallet, gently beat the thickest part until it is finer and more uniform. Butterfly breasts can also be stuffed with any filling you like.

TIPS AND TRICKS

Keeping it Clean

- Once the chicken is thawed, do not refreeze it.
- Do not allow raw chicken to come into contact with other foods, cooked or raw.
- Always wash your hands, utensils, and surfaces that have come in contact with raw chicken with hot, soapy water.
- Keep a separate cutting board for raw meat to avoid cross contamination.
- Always make sure the meat is well cooked to kill any harmful bacteria that may have been lurking.

When buying chicken

Always look for chicken that has an even colour with no blemishes or bruises. The meat should look moist and plump and have a neutral smell. Check that the packaging hasn't been damaged in any way. When buying frozen chicken, make sure that the meat is frozen solid and does not have any soft areas where it has begun to defrost – and do remember to check the sell-by-date too.

Storing Chicken

Always refrigerate or freeze chicken as soon as possible after purchasing it. If the package is damaged or soggy and you are going to cook it within two days, remove the chicken, pat dry with kitchen paper, and place on a plate. Cover with cling film or aluminum foil and place plate on bottom rack of refrigerator. That way you won't contaminate other food if it leaks. If you want to freeze the chicken at home, remove it from the package, pat dry, and seal it in an airtight bag.

TIPS AND TRICKS

Stop Breast Drying

How to stop the breast from drying out when MAKING roast chicken.
Roast the chicken breast-side down for two thirds of the cooking time. This way, all the juices will run down into the breast meat and keep it moist. Once you are ready to crisp the skin, carefully turn the chicken breast-side up and roast until golden.

How Tos and Hacks

Chicken salad. Place chicken breast side up on cutting board. Pull the the leg and thigh away from the body and use your fingers to find the hip joint in the crease. Insert the tip of a large knife into the joint and cut through the skin, meat, and joint to separate the thigh and leg from the body. Repeat on the other side. Use the same method to separate the leg from the thigh and cut the wings from the body. To remove the chicken breast, cut the breast to divide the carcass in two. Cut off all the bone and cartilage in the breasts.
You will now have two of each: thighs, drumsticks, wings, and breasts. Add the carcass to soups, stews or casseroles for flavor and remove the bones just before serving.

How to defrost a whole chicken

Thawing a frozen chicken is best done overnight in the fridge. Place it in a large bowl or on a plate to prevent the juices from dripping in the fridge. Before cooking it, check inside the cavity to see that there is no more ice. If pressed for time, put the bird in a bucket of cold water in the sink, but be sure to keep the water cold to prevent bacteria from growing.

TIPS AND TRICKS

Getting a golden skin

Check that the skin is completely dry, rub the whole bird generously with oil and season well.
Uncover the chicken 20-30 minutes before the end of the cooking time and place it on a shallow baking tray or on an oven rack on a tray to allow the dry heat to come into contact with as much skin as possible. Roast until the skin is crisp and glassy

Chicken and food poisoning

Raw chicken may contain natural bacteria, which could be dangerous if it hasn't been stored properly. Salmonella and campylobacter, which are linked to food poisoning and gastro, are among the most common.

3 DIPS FOR CHICKEN NUGGETS

Garlic and lemon mayo

Stir 2 finely chopped garlic cloves and zest and juice of 1/2 lemon into 1 cup (250 ml) Mayonnaise.

Tomato relish

Finely chop 3 small sherkins and 3 pickeled onions and stir into 3/4 cup (180ml) tomato sauce.

Sweet and sour

Stir together 3/4 cup (180 ml) pineapple juice, 1/4 cup (60 ml) apple cider vinegar, 1/4 cup (60 ml) brown sugar, 2 tbsp (30 ml) tomato cauce and 1 tbps (15 ml) cornflour. Thicker over a low heat.

Quick Recipes

Chicken Pot Pie

Simmer a couple of boneless, skinless chicken breasts, cool and dice. Microwave diced potatoes, carrots, celery, onion, green beans, or peas. Combine with cornstarch thickened chicken broth (from simmered chicken), and pour into pie crust lined baker (you can use ready-made Pillsbury), then top with the other crust, crimp, brush with milk , sprinkle with herbs, sesame seeds or a little Parmesan and bake at 350 ° for about 40 min.

Cranberry Chicken

Mix one can of whole berry cranberries w/ can of cream of mushroom soup and one packet of onion soup mix. Pour over top of chicken in baker. Cover with lid, place in oven; bake for 1-1/2 hours at 425.

Chicken and Vegetables

Place chicken (skin on or off) in baker. Place chopped onion, celery and carrots around chicken. Sprinkle with 1/2 package of Good Seasons Italian Dressing mix. Place lid on top. Bake at 350° for 1 hour.

Anatomy of the Chicken

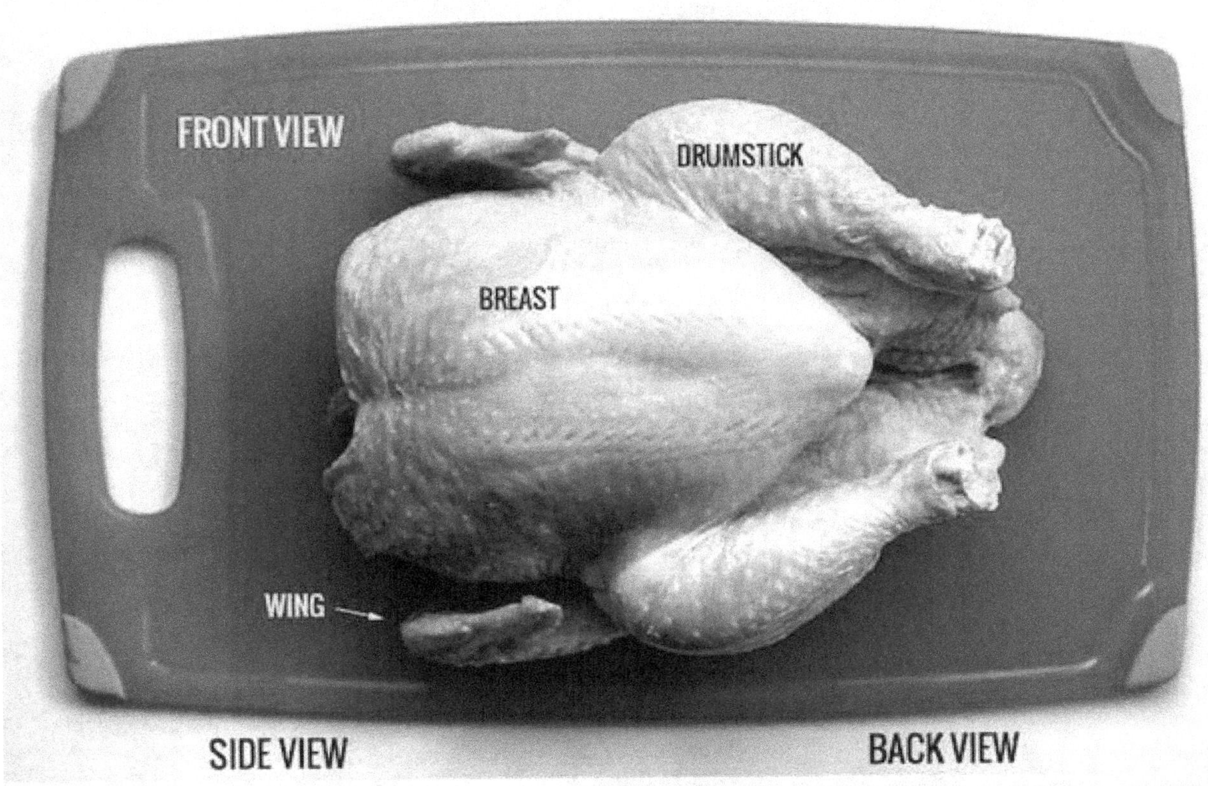
FRONT VIEW
DRUMSTICK
BREAST
WING

SIDE VIEW
WING
THIGH

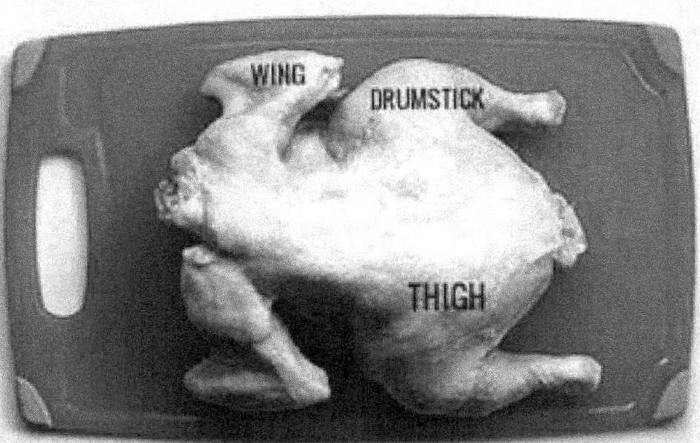
BACK VIEW
WING
DRUMSTICK
THIGH

ANATOMY OF THE CHICKEN

Head

The head is the talkie part of South Africa's famous walkie-talkies and stewing and braising are the best ways to cook it.

Breast

This very lean cut is best cooked quickly to keep them moist, for instance grilling, frying and braaiing. When stewing for braising breasts, don't overcook them as they will become dry and stringy.

Wing

Wings are high in fat and can withstand heat without becoming dry. They therefore are suited to deep- frying, braaiing and roasting. But however you cook them,

Tail

TAILS The tail is often attached to the thigh. It is packed with flavour because it contains a lot of fat and, thanks to the large skin area, becomes very crispy.

ANATOMY OF THE CHICKEN

Neck

This bony cut has very little meat but is an inexpensive way to flavour sauces and stock.

Thighs

Like drumsticks, thighs will be rather tough if not cooked properly. They have loads of fantastic flavour and are best when roasted or braised slowly or added to stews.

Drumstic

This popular cut could also be tough if it hasn't been cooked for long enough. The delicious dark brown meat particularly takes time and drumsticks taste best when they've been roasted, stewed, braised or braaied.

Feet

The other half of walkie-talkies, chicken feet are bony and low on meat. Once cooked, though, they are tender and can be eaten whole. Braai or grill them if you like crisp, crunchy skin.

HOW MANY CALORIES IN CHICKEN?

Chicken tenders

263 calories per 3.5 ounces (100 grams)

Back

137 calories per 3.5 ounces (100 grams)

Dark meat

125 calories per 3.5 ounces (100 grams)

Light meat

114 calories per 3.5 ounces (100 grams)

HOW MANY CALORIES IN CHICKEN?

Breast

A 3.5-ounce (100-gram) serving of chicken breast provides 165 calories, 31 grams of protein and 3.6 grams of fat.

Thigh

A 3.5-ounce (100-gram) serving of chicken thigh provides 209 calories, 26 grams of protein and 10.9 grams of fat.

Wing

Per 3.5 ounces (100 grams), chicken wings provide 203 calories, 30.5 grams of protein and 8.1 grams of fat.

Drumstick

Per 3.5 ounces (100 grams), chicken drumsticks have 172 calories, 28.3 grams of protein and 5.7 grams of fat.

Skin

While a skinless chicken breast is 284 calories with 80% protein and 20% fat, those numbers **dramatically** shift when you include the skin. One boneless, cooked chicken breast with skin (196 grams) contains: Calories: 386, Protein: 58.4 grams, Fat: 15.2 grams

COOKING METHODS

Grilling

This is one of the more common cooking methods, as it tends to require less added fat.

Baking or roasting

These other common methods are sufficient when you don't have access to a grill.

Broiling

This is similar to grilling, but you usually do it in a standard oven or toaster oven.

Braising

Lightly panfry the chicken and then cook it covered, submerged in liquid, for an extended time at a lower temperature.

COOKING METHODS

Fried

The chicken is submerged in hot cooking oil in either a pan or deep fryer. This creates a crisp outer coating but adds quite a bit of fat.

Baking or roasting

These other common methods are sufficient when you don't have access to a grill.

Boiling

You submerge the meat in boiling water and cook it until the internal temperature reaches 165°F (74°C). This is the leanest method, as it doesn't require added fats. Still, some may find the texture lacking.

Quick Recipes

Lemon Garlic Chicken

Place the whole roast chicken in the bakery with a whole lemon and a head of garlic (unpeeled) in the chicken cavity. Spice with salt and pepper. Cover with a lid and cook for 1-1 / 2 hours at 425 °. (Also try an orange).

Roasted Turkey Breast

Place the turkey breast in the bakery; Place 6-8 small red skinned potatoes, cut in half, around the turkey. Add 1/2 cup of white wine and 2 cloves of pressed garlic. Spice with salt and pepper. Cover with a lid. Bake at 350 ° F for 1-1 / 2 hours. Uncover for the last 15 to 20 minutes. Let stand 5 minutes before cutting.

Honey Mustard Chicken

Place the rotisserie chicken in the bakery and pour the fat-free honey mustard dressing on top. Cover with a lid. Roast 1-1 / 2 hours at 425 ° F.

3 CHEFS' TIPS
A little know-how can make life in the kitchen a lot easier

Done Yet

There are two ways to check if a chicken breast is done.
The first is to insert the tip of a small knife into the thickest part of the meat. If the juices run clear, it is cooked; if it's still pink,
you need to cook longer. Alternatively, make a small incision in the thickest part of the breast. If the meat is completely white and you don't see any pink meat, the brisket is done. The juices will also be clear. This method also works for testing whole chickens and other chicken pieces.

Slicing chicken breast for stir fry

Place the chicken breast, smooth side down, on a cutting board.
Cut diagonally into 1cm strips and cut each strip lengthwise in half into longer, thinner strips before cutting diagonally across the fibers to keep them tender.

Butterflying chicken breasts for schnitzels

Place the chicken breast smooth side down on a cutting board. Make a shallow incision along one side and continue as if you were trying to cut the breast into two identical halves. Stop just before cutting it all the way through, so the top and bottom half open like a book. With a meat mallet, tap the thickest part gently until it is finer and more uniform. Butterfly breasts can also be stuffed with any filling you like.

TIPS AND TRICKS

Keeping it Clean

- Once chicken has been defrosted, do not refreeze it.
- Don't let raw chicken come into contact with other food, cooked or uncooked.
- Always wash your hands, utensils and surfaces that have been in contact with raw chicken with hot, soapy water.
- Keep a separate chopping board for raw meat to prevent cross-contamination.
- Always make sure that meat is cooked through to kill all harmful bacteria that may have been lurking in it.

When buying chicken

Always look for chicken that has an even colour with no blemishes or bruises. The meat should look moist and plump and have a neutral smell. Check that the packaging hasn't been damaged in any way. When buying frozen chicken, make sure that the meat is frozen solid and does not have any soft areas where it has begun to defrost – and do remember to check the sell-by-date too.

Storing Chicken

Always refrigerate or freeze chicken as soon as possible after buying it. If the packet is damaged or soggy and you are going to cook it within two days, remove the chicken, pat it dry with kitchen paper and place on a plate. Cover with clingwrap or foil and put the plate on the bottom rack of the fridge. That way, it won't contaminate other food if it drips. If you want to freeze the chicken at home, remove it from the packet, pat it dry and reseal in an airtight bag.

TIPS AND TRICKS

Stop Breast Drying

How to stop the breast from drying out when MAKING roast chicken.
Roast the chicken breast-side down for two thirds of the cooking time. This way, all the juices will run down into the breast meat and keep it moist. Once you are ready to crisp the skin, carefully turn the chicken breast-side up and roast until golden.

How Tos and Hacks

Chicken salad. Place chicken breast side up on cutting board. Pull the the leg and thigh away from the body and use your fingers to find the hip joint in the crease. Insert the tip of a large knife into the joint and cut through the skin, meat, and joint to separate the thigh and leg from the body. Repeat on the other side. Use the same method to separate the leg from the thigh and cut the wings from the body. To remove the chicken breast, cut the breast to divide the carcass in two. Cut all the bone and cartilage from the breasts.
You will now have two of each: thighs, drumsticks, wings, and breasts. Add the carcass to soups, stews or casseroles for flavor and remove the bones just before serving.

How to defrost a whole chicken

Thawing a frozen chicken is best done overnight in the fridge. Place it in a large bowl or on a plate to prevent the juices from dripping in the fridge. Before cooking it, check inside the cavity to see that there is no more ice. If pressed for time, put the bird in a bucket of cold water in the sink, but be sure to keep the water cold to prevent bacteria from growing.

TIPS AND TRICKS

Getting a golden skin

Check that the skin is completely dry, rub the whole bird generously with oil and season well.
Uncover the chicken 20-30 minutes before the end of the cooking time and place it on a shallow baking tray or on an oven rack on a tray to allow the dry heat to come into contact with as much skin as possible. Roast until the skin is crisp and glassy

Chicken and food poisoning

Raw chicken may contain natural bacteria, which could be dangerous if it hasn't been stored properly. Salmonella and campylobacter, which are linked to food poisoning and gastro, are among the most common.

3 DIPS FOR CHICKEN NUGGETS

Garlic and lemon mayo

Stir 2 finely chopped garlic cloves and zest and juice of 1/2 lemon into 1 cup (250 ml) Mayonnaise.

Tomato relish

Finely chop 3 small sherkins and 3 pickeled onions and stir into 3/4 cup (180ml) tomato sauce.

Sweet and sour

Stir together 3/4 cup (180 ml) pineapple juice, 1/4 cup (60 ml) apple cider vinegar, 1/4 cup (60 ml) brown sugar, 2 tbsp (30 ml) tomato cauce and 1 tbps (15 ml) cornflour. Thicker over a low heat.

Quick Recipes

Chicken Pot Pie

Simmer a couple of boneless, skinless chicken breasts, let cool and cube. Microwave cubed potatoes, carrots, celery, onion, green beans or peas. Combine with cornstarch-thickened chicken broth (from the simmered chicken), and pour into pie crust lined baker (you can use Pillsbury ready made) then top with the other crust, crimp, brush with milk, sprinkle with herbs, sesame seeds, or a little Parmesan, and bake at 350° about 40 min.

Cranberry Chicken

Mix one can of whole berry cranberries w/ can of cream of mushroom soup and one packet of onion soup mix. Pour over top of chicken in baker. Cover with lid, place in oven; bake for 1-1/2 hours at 425.

Chicken and Vegetables

Place chicken (skin on or off) in baker. Place chopped onion, celery and carrots around chicken. Sprinkle with 1/2 package of Good Seasons Italian Dressing mix. Place lid on top. Bake at 350° for 1 hour.

5 TIPS FOR GRILLED CHICKEN

Use bone in skin on chicken pieces

The thighs are highly recommended by grill experts, and I agree they are the most humid, but the legs, breasts, and wings also benefit when the bones and skin are left intact, as they help insulate the meat from overcooked and make it taste so much better.

(However, if you're committed to boneless, skinless chicken breasts, the techniques you practice with the remaining tips will help you master them with practice, too).

Pasture-raised chickens, especially those of traditional breeds, are not only tastier but also more sustainable than factory-farmed poultry, so look for them in your area at the farmer's market or local grocery store.

5 TIPS FOR GRILLED CHICKEN

Season chicken well with salt

Most people make their first mistake even before turning on the grill: they don't season the chicken enough.

Using your best quality kosher or sea salt, sprinkle all sides of the chicken pieces as if you were finely dusting them with powdered sugar.

Everyone loves marinated chicken, but dipping it into any sauce, even barbecue sauce, will bring you more cooking complications, not more flavor.

5 TIPS FOR GRILLED CHICKEN

Preheat your grill and flames under control

A diferencia de otros alimentos que responden bien al calor intenso, el pollo requiere un calor moderado o medio-alto (entre 350 F y 400 F).

Ya sea que use una parrilla de carbón o de gas, pruebe los patrones de calor colocando su palma abierta a unas 5 pulgadas por encima de la parrilla.

Si puede mantenerlo allí durante 5 segundos, está dentro del alcance.

También tenga en cuenta dónde el calor es menos intenso.

En caso de un brote, mueva inmediatamente el pollo a estas partes más frías de la parrilla para evitar que se queme.

5 TIPS FOR GRILLED CHICKEN

Brown chicken pieces skin side down

Always cook chicken skin side down first and plan to leave it there for the next 20 minutes or more, or until almost fully cooked.

Why? You'll end up with a crisp, beautifully browned skin (remember, isolate the meat), plus the chicken will cook evenly to the bone.

In general, it takes at least 30 minutes to cook bone-in chicken to this temperature, so try to cook it skin side down for three-quarters of the total cooking time (20 to 25 minutes) before turning. and finish it in the second. side.

5 TIPS FOR GRILLED CHICKEN

Use your grill as an oven

After placing the chicken pieces on the grill, cover.

Now your grill will radiate heat both up and down, which is exactly what your chicken needs to get fully cooked.

The lid also controls airflow and prevents the flames of a charcoal grill from getting out of control.

Fat dripping will likely cause breakouts, so monitor cooking and move chicken away from flames into cooler areas of the grill when necessary.

If you are not sure if the chicken is done, insert the tip of an instant read thermometer close to the bone or just cut in the center for a visual check.

The 5 Most Common Grilled Chicken Mistakes

Mistake n. 1
Not knowing the right cooking temperature for chicken

Mistake n. 2
Cooking too hot, lead to raw chicken too quickly

Mistake n. 3
Turn the chicken to the grill marks and get a blaze instead

Mistake n. 4
Finish with hard, dry chicken

Mistake n. 5
Grilled Chicken Sticks

The Great Chicken

USE SKIN-ON-BONE CHICKEN

The skin protects the meat from drying out and, along with the bone, adds a ton of flavor. Also, this method does not work with boneless, skinless chicken, which should be grilled quickly over high heat.

GET OUT OF THE COLD

Remove the chicken from the refrigerator and let it spread out at room temperature while the grill heats up. If the chicken is too cold when it hits the hot grill, the meat will tighten and become tough and may remain cold and raw near the bone even after the rest is well cooked.

MARINATE FOR EXTRA GOODNESS

You don't have to marinate, but if you do, you'll be rewarded with tastier meat. Marino at room temperature while the grill heats up. Enough time to season the meat (soaking chicken in sour marinades can make the consistency doughy). If you want to skip the marinade, sprinkle the chicken generously with kosher salt before letting it sit at room temperature.

MAKE SURE THE GRILL IS AT THE RIGHT TEMPERATURE

You want moderately high heat that registers 400 degrees on a built-in thermometer when the lid is closed. Turn the knobs on a gas grill between the highest and medium setting. On a charcoal grill, distribute the incinerated coals in an even layer. The coals are ready when you can hold your hand a thumb above the grill for 3 seconds before instinctively walking away.

PREPARE THE CHICKEN SKIN

Just before placing the chicken on the grill, wipe off the excess marinade, then pull the chicken skin over the meat to cover it as much as possible. If there is extra skin on the thighs (lucky!), Wrap it over the skinless parts. This will help the skin brown evenly and keep the meat more tender. Place the chicken on the hot grill with the skin side down.

DO NOT MOVE THE MEAT

Cover the grill, opening the top vents on a charcoal grill. In this first stage of cooking, you want the skin to turn a deep golden brown. When ready, it will naturally break free from the grill. If it starts to brown too quickly, lower the heat. If you try to flip it over and it clings to the grill, let it sit longer.

TASTE THE MEAT

After flipping the chicken, cook it skin side up until the meat is almost cooked if you are going to glaze it and if not, it is fully cooked. To test the doneness, slide a sharp kitchen knife close to the bone. It should slide in and out easily and the blade should be hot. Any juices that run out should be clear. If you have an accurate meat thermometer, meat close to the bone should register 160 degrees for bone-in breasts and 165 degrees for dark meat.

GLASS EVENLY AND FINISH

COOKING

If you are glazing the chicken with the sauce, brush the skin with a generous layer when the meat is almost cooked (155 degrees for the brisket; 160 for the legs). Turn it over and brush the other side. Continue glazing and brushing at a steady pace until the chicken has a coat of caramelized sauce.

WAIT FOR IT

When you take the chicken off the grill, you'll be drooling from its smoky scent. But resist the temptation to do it right away. Let the chicken rest on the uncovered tray for about five minutes before serving. This will make the meat juicier and let the glaze soak up its flavor.

USE SKIN-ON-BONE CHICKEN

The skin protects the meat from drying out and, along with the bone, adds a ton of flavor. Also, this method does not work with boneless, skinless chicken, which should be grilled quickly over high heat.

GET OUT OF THE COLD

Remove the chicken from the refrigerator and let it spread out at room temperature while the grill heats up. If the chicken is too cold when it hits the hot grill, the meat will tighten and become tough and may remain cold and raw near the bone even after the rest is well cooked.

MARINATE FOR EXTRA GOODNESS

You don't have to marinate, but if you do, you'll be rewarded with tastier meat. Marino at room temperature while the grill heats up. Enough time to season the meat (soaking chicken in sour marinades can make the consistency doughy). If you want to skip the marinade, sprinkle the chicken generously with kosher salt before letting it sit at room temperature.

MAKE SURE THE GRILL IS AT THE RIGHT TEMPERATURE

You want moderately high heat that registers 400 degrees on a built-in thermometer when the lid is closed. Turn the knobs on a gas grill between the highest and medium setting. On a charcoal grill, distribute the incinerated coals in an even layer. The coals are ready when you can hold your hand a thumb above the grill for 3 seconds before instinctively walking away.

PREPARE THE CHICKEN SKIN

Just before placing the chicken on the grill, wipe off the excess marinade, then pull the chicken skin over the meat to cover it as much as possible. If there is extra skin on the thighs (lucky!), Wrap it over the skinless parts. This will help the skin brown evenly and keep the meat more tender. Place the chicken on the hot grill with the skin side down.

DO NOT MOVE THE MEA

Cover the grill, opening the top vents on a charcoal grill. In this first stage of cooking, you want the skin to turn a deep golden brown. When ready, it will naturally break free from the grill. If it starts to brown too quickly, lower the heat. If you try to flip it over and it clings to the grill, let it sit longer.

TASTE THE MEAT

After flipping the chicken, cook it skin side up until the meat is almost cooked if you are going to glaze it and if not, it is fully cooked. To test the doneness, slide a sharp kitchen knife close to the bone. It should slide in and out easily and the blade should be hot. Any juices that run out should be clear. If you have an accurate meat thermometer, meat close to the bone should register 160 degrees for bone-in breasts and 165 degrees for dark meat.

GLASS EVENLY AND FINISH COOKING

If you are glazing the chicken with the sauce, brush the skin with a generous layer when the meat is almost cooked (155 degrees for the brisket; 160 for the legs). Turn it over and brush the other side. Continue glazing and brushing at a steady pace until the chicken has a coat of caramelized sauce.

CPSIA information can be obtained
at www.ICGtesting.com
Printed in the USA
BVHW010852150621
609627BV00003B/283